62 YEARS ON

From 1st Radio to the 373rd ISRG, the complete chronology of the Air Force at Misawa's Security Hill with photos

by Lee Martin

1

Dedication

This book is dedicated to the silent sentinels who labored in anonymity on The Hill all the while making the world a safer place through their vigilance. It was an honor and privilege to be a member of this elite group.

Dear reader: if you also worked on The Hill, thank you for your dedication to the mission. To other veterans, thank you for your service.

Table of Contents

Forward

The following work is a pictorial walk down memory lane covering the 62 and one half years of "Freedom Through Vigilance" by the U.S. Air Force on Misawa's Security Hill.

Part 1, the history, addresses the organizations, facilities and people that occupied The Hill for 62 and a half years. Emphasis is on the units assigned to The Hill but only pertains to their time at Misawa. Often units can be deactivated and then later reactivated at some other location. I have included some information on the facilities on The Hill as well as some significant accomplishments of people that made The Hill come to life. Finally, you will find information concerning units that comprise the rest of Misawa Air Base, both U.S. and Japanese, as well as landmark events affecting the local area as they pertain to the established timeline. Some of the photos are quite old and a little grainy. I did as much as I could to clean them up and I apologize in advance.

Part 2 is a list of unit awards earned by the various Air Force organizations while they were assigned to Misawa.

Part 3 is a list of The Hill's host unit commanders.

Part 4 is a short list of "Do You Remember" items that may evoke some pleasurable memories.

As an added bonus, at the end of the book you will find a link to my website that contains a compilation of photos of The Hill and Misawa that did not fit into the actual book due to the sheer size of the files. I include them because I feel may evoke a few *natsukashi (*good old days) memories.

Preface

I'm told by folks who should know that Security Hill was not actually a hill. It has a lower elevation than the main base. However, as Hill vets know, when transiting the access road between the lakes to get to there, you have to drive, pedal, walk, run, etc. up an incline that leads to The Hill. Anyway, the name is carved in stone, as it should be.

So why did I choose Misawa for this endeavor and not one of the other equally important cryptologic sites around the world? Simple; I'm in Misawa, have been here for over 30 years and spent 13 of my 24 years in USAFSS/ESC on Security Hill. I'm extremely proud to say that I worked on The Hill and its closure has significant emotional meaning to me.

At some point along your way through this material, you will probably deduce that I am not a very good writer. Guilty as charged! But my aim is not to produce an award-winning historical masterpiece. My goal is to depict The Hill, Misawa AB and the Misawa area as the great place I believe it to be and in a way that will bring back some great memories for those of you who spent time in Misawa. The data contained herein is a result of years of research and is accurate to the best of my knowledge.

Manned collection, analysis and reporting took place for 60 and one half years, January 1953 to July 2013. However, after a great deal of thought, I decided to include the period through July 2015 because, while the nuts and bolts of the mission moved in 2013, the military cryptologic presence (parent unit and the support squadron) remained to ensure proper disposition of all the mission assets that remained when the operators and analysts departed. This included the razing of the FLR-9, the reutilization or disposal of all the sensitive equipment and the smooth turnover of the remaining assets to the civilian agency that is responsible for taking care of the remaining assets.

Materials used to compile this unofficial chronology include a thorough and time consuming perusal of the Wingspread and Northern Light base newspaper archives, the internet, printed works available at the base library (including an unpublished but informative pamphlet from the 1970s by John L. Arata), input from the 301st IS 60th Anniversary Committee, the 301st IS Inactivation Committee, the usafssmisawa.com web site, the Air Force Personnel Center's "AwardsDMZ" website, the "homeofheros" website, photographic skills of SFC Ronald Stark (Ret) U.S. Army and numerous unknown photographers who posted graphics online, the amazing memory of SMSgt Cecil Hahn (Ret) and my own memory (what's left of it) based on my 30+ years here at Misawa. I'd like to thank everyone who provided information to supplement my own experiences.

I have one last disclaimer. There are some periods in the history of The Hill where my research yielded conflicting information. I did the best I could to sort out all the discrepancies that I found. That being said, I will warn you that, here and there, a date or some other fact may be slightly off due to conflicting historical accounts. All that being said, let's begin our trip down memory lane. Enjoy!

Introduction

I guess you could say it all started back in 1931 when Clyde Pangborn and Hugh Herndon took off from Misawa's Sabishiro Beach in a single-engine monoplane and arrived in Wenatchee, Washington 41 hours later, thus completing history's first non-stop trans-pacific flight. While there was no base here at the time, this is the first noted activity in Misawa's aviation history.

In 1935 the Imperial Japanese Army began construction of an airfield near Lake Ogawara in Misawa. In 1942, the Imperial Japanese Navy assumed control of the recently completed base and hosted long-range bombers that were intended to launch attacks against the United States. However, these attacks never happened and the base was mostly used for training sorties. Near the end of the war, one Kamikaze unit deployed from here.

On 14 September 1945 the U.S. Army's 32nd Engineering Construction Group under the command of Captain Davis K. Stark occupied and began rebuilding the base. Training, gunnery and bombing ranges used by the Japanese were also taken over by U.S. troops. In December of 1946, the U.S. Army Air Corps' 49th Fighter Group became the first U.S. air unit assigned to Misawa.

First U.S. base commander

The signing of the National Security Act by President Truman in July 1947 created the U.S. Air Force and 13 months later the Air Force officially assumed control of Misawa Air Base.

In 1950 the population of Misawa was 24,790 souls.

In September 1951 the U.S. and Japan signed a formal Peace Treaty and the U.S. occupation of Japan (excluding Okinawa) ended. Many U.S. forces remained in place and fell under the terms of the Security Treaty between Japan and America and the 6016th Air Base Wing took control of Misawa Air Base. The main units assigned to Misawa were the Army's 753 AAA Gun Battalion which included A, B C and D Batteries and, as of 1953, the Air Force's 39th Air Division flying F84s and F86s.

The base newspaper, The Wingspread, published its first issue in January 1952. It and its successor, The Northern Light, were extremely helpful in my research for this book.

On a different front, back at Fort George Wright, Washington in January 1942, the U.S. Army's 138th Signal Radio Intelligence Company was born. In 1945 (or 1946 as I found conflicting information) the unit was renamed the 1st Radio Squadron Mobile (RSM).

U.S. Army 1st RSM Patch

U.S. Army's 1st Radio Squadron Mobile

In 1949 the 1st RSM was transferred to the U.S. Air Force.

1st Radio Squadron Mobile Patch

History

In April 1951 the fledgling United States Air Force Security Service (USAFSS) performed a number of hearability and feasibility tests on a small piece of land that was physically separated from Misawa Air Base's flight line and the rest of the main base area by Lake Anenuma and Lake Ogawara. A permanent detachment was in place by the end of the year.

On 1 September 1951 USAFSS activated the 6920th Security Group (SG) at Johnson AB, Japan, responsible for managing USAFSS operations in the Far East and performing second echelon analysis for subordinate units. The 6920th moved to Shiroi AB a few miles from Johnson in 1954. The unit eventually relocated to Hawaii in 1958. The stage was set for the activation of the full-blown unit at Misawa.

Below are some of the fine accommodations that the early Hill personnel were blessed with.

Early Accomodations on Security Hill

Autumn 1952 – 1ˢᵗ Radio Sqdn. Mobile (Detachment 11)
(Near) Misawa Air Force Base
The "My Home" notation is from the photographer, not me.

The word "near" in the description of the above photo refers to the fact that what became Security Hill was not officially a part of the base at the time (as far as I was able to determine).

other bARRACKS AND A Com bldg
No one was allowed around
except operATORS,

11

On 26 January 1953 the 1st RSM under the command of Lt. Col Charles Sheppard moved to Misawa from Johnson Air Base as a field station under the 6920th SG. The unit took up residency on this patch of land northwest of main base and became known as Security Hill. The rest is interesting history.

In November of that year, the 49th Fighter-Bomber Wing was activated at Misawa.

In July 1954 the Self-Defense Forces of Japan were organized under the Defense Agency with three main branches; Air, Maritime and Ground Self-Defense Forces. The Japanese Air Self-Defense Forces (JASDF) activated the Northern Aircraft Control Training Squadron as their first unit at Misawa Air Base in October of 1954.

The base was obviously growing and becoming a significant part of the U.S. presence in the strategic area of northern Japan. Below are some photos from a few 1954 editions of the Wingspread.

The Airmen's Club

Base Beach on what we now call Lake Ogawara

Rocker Club (NCO Club)

On 8 May 1955 the 1st RSM became the 6921st RSM. I find it interesting that as late as the 1970s some Japanese, especially taxi drivers, still referred to The Hill as 1st Radio.

Also in 1955 the 6139th Air Base Group took over as host of the base.

In January of 1956 the Wingspread published a pay chart that showed an E1 under two years of service received $78 per month and an E9 under two years of service (how is that possible?) received $400.

On 5 May 1956 a fire destroyed the Officers' Club. Luckily, no one was injured.

In July of 1956 the 6921st RSM was re-designated the 6921st Radio Group Mobile (RGM). Along with this change the 6989th RSM was activated at Misawa and the 6986th RSM at Wakkanai, Japan and both were subordinate to the 6921st RGM.

Original Operations Building (Bldg. S-1555)

Welcome to The Hill - 1957

6921st RGM Patch – 1957

JASDF remained a key player at Misawa as they activated the Headquarters, Northern Air Defense Division in July of 1957.

The 6989th Support Squadron (Spt. Sq.) was activated at Misawa on 1 July 1958 also under the 6921st RGM. (Note: I found conflicting information in my research. The activation of the 6989th Spt. Sq. may have occurred in 1956 in conjunction with the activation the 6989th SS. For those who were here at the time, I apologize if I got it backwards.)

In 1958 FEN Misawa switched to 1580 KHz and the base purchased 900 Sakura (flowering cherry) trees and planted them around the base. This is what they look like in 2015:

15

Sakura in Flag Circle (now Riesner Circle) with F4 Static Display – 2015

July of 1958 saw the activation of the 21st Tactical Fighter Wing (TFW). The wing's 531st TFS introduced the F100 Super Saber and, in October, the 45th Tactical Reconnaissance Squadron brought their F101 Voodoos. The F84s were phased out as the newer aircraft replaced them.

In 1958 the 753rd AAA Gun Battalion relinquished the area that hosted its B Battery to the Japanese government. The area soon started blooming with housing and became the famous B Battery housing area where many Hill folks lived.

The 50s also saw a building boom on The Hill as you can see by the below aerial photo of The Hill taken in 1958. Dorms and a theater, a bank branch and a small BX and more sprang up on the Hill and it eventually became like its own small base.

1958 aerial photo of The Hill

Engineering Diagram of The Hill late 50s.

17

The Static Club opened on The Hill in December 1958. Airman 3rd Class Botarez won a bottle of bourbon for submitting the winning name for the facility. The club is shown in the photo below.

In 1959 two F51 Mustangs collided over the Misawa flight line and crashed onto the aircraft parking apron destroying a total of 14 aircraft.

By 1960 the population of Misawa had risen dramatically to over 38 thousand. FEN Misawa gave the base population a Christmas present with the broadcast of the first American TV programs on new UHF Channel 73.

1961 turned out to be no different than the last few years as the base continued to grow. JASDF activated the Northern Civil Engineering Squadron and the Northern Aircraft Control and Warning Wing which assumed aircraft control operations for the region. In Feb of 61 the first F102 Delta Dagger was accepted by the U.S. 4th Fighter Interceptor Squadron. This marked the beginning of the end for the venerable F86 for U.S. forces at Misawa.

In 1961 the cost of a haircut on base went from a quarter to 30 cents. The first price increase since 1946.

In May of 1961 two Technical Sergeants from The Hill, A.C. Chamblee and John L. Sinnard began a charitable organization to be operated by the 6989th

SS to provide financial assistance in support of the blind and deaf in the area. They joined with Dr. Kitesu Imaizumi of the Iwate Medical Center and together they funded a number of successful corneal transplants. This charity continued operation right up until the units on The Hill started shutting things down 54 years later. It's a shame that the unit is gone but it's also a shame that such a long history of giving goes away as well. For more info on how Eyesight got its start, please check out John Sinnard's story at

http://www.usafssmisawa.com/prd/mem-stories.php?idx=operationeyesight.

Operation Eyesight Lapel Pin

World Record Softball Fundraiser

Eyesight Children – 2011

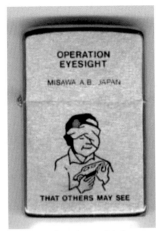

Eyesight Zippo Lighter

On 1 September 1962, the 6921st RGM was redesignated the 6921st Security Wing (SW). I was unable to find a shield for the unit. Below is what the USAFSS shield looked like in 1962.

Also in Sep of 62, U.S. troops in Japan stopped receiving Military Payment Certificates (MPC) for the values of U.S. coins. They now receive actual pennies, nickels, dimes and quarters in their financial transactions. It's also about this time that the off-base area becomes Misawa City; not O-Misawa. Furamagi, and other smaller entities. The city is incorporating and growing.

When you came in the main gate in the early 1960s, this is what you passed through. It's kind of hard to tell where the actual checkpoint was but it was there someplace in the right center area of the photo.

Construction of the FLR 9 antenna ("Elephant Cage") began in 1963 and was completed in 1965 at a cost of over $3.3 million. As an old DF'er I can tell you that the full name of the Cage was "Army Navy/Fixed Radio Receiving 9, Variable" (AN/FLR9-V). The new operations building, Bldg. 1500, was also constructed during this period.

FLR-9 under construction

This antenna revolutionized the HF mission at Misawa and became famous in the area. Over the years, there were numerous myths and guesses as to its function.

In the early 70s, there was talk that some local Japanese believed that the A and B band elements of the antenna were missiles. This belief may have stemmed in part from Misawa's history of Anti-Aircraft Artillery (AAA) batteries around the base. These batteries were deactivated in the mid-1950s. Many of you who lived off-base lived in B Battery (the area that once held the actual AAAs B Battery). In addition, these elements were cylindrical, stood in a vertical position and the top of the towers had a cone-shaped cap. The fact that there was a tall pole-like feature coming out of the top of the element didn't seem to deter this notion.

Aerial view of the completed FLR 9

Ground level view of the completed FLR 9

In 1963, the 6989th RSM became the 6989th SS.

I didn't reach my first field unit until 1969 but I remember the equipment shown in the photo below. I guess that the configuration of these collection positions seen in this photo must have been around the mid-60s. I don't see a PT-6 recorder on these positions and the ops are sitting alongside their radios instead of facing between the racks. I do remember the 6-ply paper, though.

In January 1964 the base underwent another change of command as the 439th Combat Support Group became the host unit.

In October 1964, the 6989th SS was inactivated leaving the 6921st SW as the lone unit in Operations and the 6989th Spt. Gp. remained active.

In March of 1965, the FLR-9 Antenna became operational and the move from building 1555 to 1500 began. This was completed and bldg. 1500 became the Ops building in May of 1965. Below is photo of the "Key to the FLR" being presented.

In April of 1965 the 6921st SW lost control of The Hill's mail room. The facility stayed on The Hill but it became subordinate to the base Post Office.

I guess I was a bit naïve but I was surprised to find that other units used the R-390 radio. The photo below is from the Wingspread and shows the Far East Network using them.

In July of '65, the 6921st SW/Shift 3 (sic) set a world record for a marathon softball game. They played for 70 hours logging 435 innings. The score was Dots 522 and Dashes 487. I love the play on the ditty bop theme. They earned $500 which was donated to Operation Eyesight. Dr. Iwaizumi, the eye surgeon who performed the eye surgeries that Eyesight sponsored threw out the first pitch. (I wonder if the flights were known as "shifts" during this time or did the paper misspeak).

In November 1965, the main base's two permanent party F100 squadrons departed Misawa for good, significantly reducing the main base population. They were replaced by F100 units that deployed on a rotational basis from the CONUS (Continental United States).

On 11 January 1966 a major fire destroyed a large portion of Misawa City. 45 MPH winds spread the fire over 20 blocks of the downtown area destroying 275 buildings with an estimated damage of over $4 million (1966 dollars). Over 2000 base personnel including many from The Hill assisted the firefighting and recovery efforts. The base provided one of its aircraft hangers as an emergency shelter. The following year, three Hill members were awarded the Air Force Commendation Medal for their efforts during the tragedy.

The aftermath of the 1966 Fire

Summer of '66 also marked the 5-year anniversary of Operation Eyesight. During that period, Eyesight paid for 50 successful vision-restoration surgeries.

In July of that year, The Hill decided to take a shot at regaining the world record for marathon softball, which had apparently been taken from them. The game lasted 90 hours and spanned 462 innings. The final score was Record Breakers – 608 and the Misawans – 444. Eight of the original

27

starters of the game played all 462 innings. Seeing as how this event took place if late June, they played entire game in heavy mist and fog that naturally comes with Misawa's rainy season. They also raised $1500 for Operation Eyesight.

Finally in 1966, the Wingspread announced in print that their pages would no longer feature "pin-up girls".

In August of 1967, The Hill Post Office got its own APO number thereby making it a full-fledged Air Post Office. Do you remember APO 96210?

In October of '67 the first F4 Phantom fighter aircraft arrived at Misawa to join the 356th TFS and replace the aging F100s. Additional Phantoms arrived later in the month and on into the remainder of the year.

Also in October of this year, the Air Force changed the name and designation of the E-4 pay grade. E-4s became Sergeants instead of Airman First Class and were awarded all the authority, responsibilities and prestige of the NCO ranks. The names of the E1 through E3 also changed. They became Airman Basic, Airman and Airman First Class, respectively.

At 9:50am on 16 May 1968 Misawa experienced the second major disaster in just over two years. "Great Shakes Day" was the eventual nickname given to the day a major earthquake centered in the Pacific Ocean just off the east coast of Misawa killed 27, injured 210 and left 10 missing in the northern Japan area. Roads buckled, buildings collapsed, railroad tracks twisted in strange directions and crevices appeared in the earth. Fortunately, there were no casualties among base personnel. There have been other earthquakes over the years but none have done anywhere near the damage in Misawa of the 1968 shaker. (I was unable to find the final disposition of the 10 missing folks cited above.)

The aftermath of the 1968 quake.

During this time The Hill had its own dormitories. Here is a shot of most of the dorms taken from the water tower.

View of The Hill Dorms in 1970 taken from the water tower.

In the above photo, the building in the foreground center and its wing on the right was the original dining hall which became the Static Club when the original club building closed and then the Navy admin section. Dorm 4 has only the end of the building showing at the left foreground. In the early 70s, that was the women's dorm. Behind it are Dorms 5 and 6 (my dorm from 70 – 72). Across the street is the Glenn Dining Hall and the rest of the dorms are behind it and across the street in the upper left. By the turn of the century, all the dorms were gone as well as the circuit breaker, linen exchange and library.

Also in 1968, the 39th Air Division was redesignated as the 475th Tactical Fighter Wing (TFW). All the subordinate units on main base also assumed the 475th designation except the Comm. Sq. It remained the 1961 Communications Squadron.

In August of '68, 2Lt Rachel Mullins became the first woman (WAF was the term used at the time) assigned to The Hill. She served as an Intel Officer in Operations. Then in September A1C Bonnie Olson became the first enlisted woman assigned to The Hill and she worked in the in- and out-processing section of The Hill's Combined Base Personnel Office.

The Circuit Breaker, The Hill's gym/recreation center, opened its doors to Hill personnel in September as well.

In 1969 the 6989th Spt. Sq. became the 6921st Spt. Sq.

In the late 60s and early 70s improved technology led to base closings all over Japan. Wakkanai AS and Chitose AB on Hokkaido, Tachikawa AB in Tokyo and Naha on Okinawa as well as other smaller installations are closed outright or given over to JASDF but Misawa was spared. Many of these bases had a USAFSS presence. Misawa picked up some of the mission and personnel from a couple of these bases.

On 1 April 1970 the 6921st SW became the 6921st SG and the 6921st Support Group was deactivated.

Aerial photo of the Ops portion of The Hill – 1970

In March, 1970 the 16th TRS arrived in Misawa serving the 475th TFW. This provided the wing a dedicated airborne tactical reconnaissance capability.

In 1970 the military population of Misawa Air Base was at its highest level ever with 6,000 GIs on the base. I arrived in September of this year and according to my feeble memory, there were over 1,000 Air Force folks working on The Hill. Each flight consisted of over 200 airmen. But these numbers are soon to change.

The U.S. Army presence on The Hill began in September of 1970 when the Army Security Agency opened U.S. Army Field Station, Misawa. As far as I can tell, they had about 130 personnel assigned.

In addition, in March 1971 the 475th TFW was deactivated at Misawa and moved to Kunsan Air Base in South Korea and took all of their F4s with them. The 6112th ABG was simultaneously activated and took over as host at Misawa. Most of the main base units fell under the 6112th but some of them became subordinate to the newly activated Detachment 1, 374th ABW at Yokota AB, located near Tokyo. By the way, JASDF is flying F104s during this time frame.

Also in March of 1971, the Wingspread base newspaper ceased publication and was replaced by the Northern Light.

In 1 July 1971, the U.S. Navy Security Group Activity Misawa was established and in October Company E Marine detachment arrived to share space as a tenant unit in the gig, as the operations building was referred to.

Another sure sign that things were changing was President Nixon "floating" the dollar in August of 71. For the first time since April 1949, the yen sank below 360 to the U.S. dollar. Those of us who were in Misawa at the time will never forget that dark day. By 1 December 2012 the exchange rate sank to 73 to the dollar.

1971 – Welcome Marquee - Dorm and water tower in background

Below are some of the flight/trick patches in use during the early to mid-1970s.

When Brady AS in Hakata on the island of Kyushu joined the growing list of closed facilities in 1972, Misawa absorbed a lot of their mission and personnel and that bumped manning up again.

Here is a look at some of the equipment in use in the 70s.

OPSCOMM (Operations Communications)

OPSCOMM Mod-28 Teletype

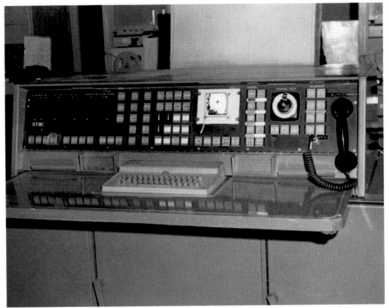

URC-53 Communication Position

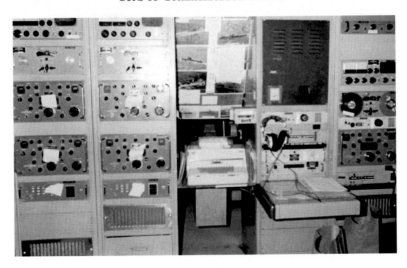

Collection positions
(R390 radios, AG-22 teletypewriter, PT6 Recorder, headsets, FLR9 antenna selector panel, intercom)

The photo above could be a Manual Morse or Voice collection position. The photo is taken from the Heritage Hall display and the display calls it Comfy Dinosaur.

On 1 July 1972 the 6112th ABG was deactivated and USAFSS activated the 6920th ABG to take over host responsibilities for Misawa Air Base. This marks the first and only time since the Army left and the Air Force took over the base in 1948 that Misawa Air Base was under a major command other than Pacific Air Forces (PACAF) and there were no U.S. Air Force aircraft assigned. I stood the change of command ceremony. The unit performing the mission on The Hill remained the 6921st SG.

The first woman assigned to an operational flight arrived sometime in 1972. I am not sure of the date and try as I might, I cannot find any reference to it. Anyway, the first woman to actually sit rack on the Ops Floor was Airman (A1C?) Karen Morrow. She was a 292X1 assigned to Trick 4 (as was I).

Then on 1 September of '72, the 6921st SG on The Hill was redesignated the 6921st SW and the 6920th ABG became subordinate to it.

During this time frame, the original operations building, building 1555, functioned as the Community Center. It contained The Hill Post Office, BX, bank, snack bar, chapel, sick call room, etc. and, if you were here during that time, you will remember the embroidery shop that did such a great job producing morale caps, morale jackets, bowling shirts and more. Below is a photo of two such Morale Jackets and a bowling shirt. You can tell by the colors that the one on the top is from Trick 1 (Able Flight) and the other is from Trick 4 (Dawg Flight). Trick 2 (Baker Flight) used blue and Trick 3 (Charlie Flight) wore red. The sleeves would have had patches of all the places they were stationed. The other sleeve would probably have had a patch or the name of their home state. Various other data was often included. The bowling shirt is older as you can see it is from the 6989th RSM

On 5 February 1973, Sgt. Joseph Matejov, a 292X1 with whom I served on Trick 4, and been reassigned to Vietnam died when his EC47 aircraft was shot down over Vietnam. He is the only person who had ever been assigned to Misawa's Security Hill to die in combat in Vietnam. The unit would later honor him in a memorialization ceremony. We'll discuss it further along in the timeline.

39

I departed Misawa at the end of my first tour in September of 1973.

Misawa Main Gate – 1973

In July 1974 the 6920th SG was activated to maintain the mission on The Hill and joined the 6920th AGB under the 6921SW.

1974 closed with the rising value of the yen giving the base population only 293 to the dollar.

Folks coming to or leaving Misawa will no longer have to bounce around the sky in the old DC4. World Airways begins 727 jet service between Misawa and Yokota Air Base which is outside Tokyo.

The Naval Security Group Misawa was awarded the prestigious Travis Trophy for 1975. This award is given by the National Security Agency for the most outstanding Service Cryptologic Unit for the year.

Also in 1975 someone decided that a new E4 should not be considered an NCO after all. So another confusing decree split the pay grade into E4 Apprentice and E4 NCO. A new E4 would hold the apprentice designation for period of one year and during that year, undergo supervisory training. Then, when all requirements were met, he or she magically became E4 NCO (or E4 Sergeant). Then in order to distinguish the rank insignia between the two, the Apprentice wore three stripes without the star in the center. The E2 and E3 stripes also lost their star. Whew!

The Airman's Club was closed in 1975 and Airmen were authorized to use the old Rocker Club which had been the NCO Club. The building was remodeled and became the Tohoku Enlisted Club open to all enlisted ranks.

On 1 Feb 1976, the 6921st SW became the 6920th SW. The 6920th SG taking care of operations and the 6920th ABG running the main base remained subordinate to it. This marked the deactivation of the 6921st unit designator. (I found one source that said this happened in 1974 so there is a conflict. However, I believe 1976 is correct.)

Here are a few more patches I was able to uncover, mostly thanks to the USAFSS in Misawa web site. You would have seen these on morale jackets in the late 70s and into the 80s. The exception is the 6989th SS Trick1 patch which is circa 1964.

In July of 1977, after only 10 years in business, Operation Eyesight provided funds for a successful surgical procedure for its 100th patient. Also in the summer of 1977, the base paper began referring to the shifts as Able, Baker, Charlie and Dawg flight instead of Trick 1, 2, 3 and 4 (sigh).

On 1 Oct 1978 control of the base reverted back to PACAF. The 6920th SW and the 6920th ABG were retired on 29 September. The 6920th SG up on The Hill was redesignated the 6920th SS. The 6112th Air Base Group was activated and assumes the host role for PACAF.

On 1 August 1979 United States Air Force Security Service became the Electronic Security Command and the 6920th SS became the 6920th Electronic Security Group (ESG).

New ESC Shield

I can't find the exact dates but it was about this time when many of us had our AFSCs change. The 292XX became 207XX and some 208XX variants became 203XX.

In 1979, JASDF converts to the Mitsubishi F-1 as their main fighter in Misawa.

Bldg. 1500 in the late 70s.

In 1980, the unit hosted it's first-ever Spouse Open House and family members were escorted in the gig and given the unclassified briefing.

1980's census figures showed 40,165 folks living in Misawa City. The military population was down to almost half of its 1970 size and sits at 3,100. You could only get 203 yen for one U.S. dollar.

Sometime around 1980, Operation Eyesight no longer had the need to subsidize eye surgeries. The government of Japan began including blind and deaf patients in the Standard Japanese Health Insurance program (that's how it was explained to me when I became president of Eyesight in the mid '80s). This had been one of Eyesight's original goals. However, the group was still active and provided funds to the Hachinohe School for the Blind and Deaf. These funds were used to purchase specialty items such braille typewriters, medical equipment and other such equipment needed by the school.

Aerial View of Misawa City and the base, circa 1980.
A portion of The Hill is cut off in the upper left of the shot.

In early 1981 Col Alan T. Smith, The Hill commander, finally displayed the new 6920th ESG shield. Here it is:

Ne Plus Ultra

In August of 1981, the contract is awarded for construction of the first "Golf Ball" Geodesic Satellite antenna on Security Hill.

Also in August of 81, JASDF started flying the E2C early warning aircraft.

Late March 1981 – melting snow and soft mud at Misawa's main gate. The transition from winter to spring was usually messy.

Main Gate – 1981

45

In January 1982, building 672, a new dormitory for Hill personnel, opened on main base. 390 hill residents moved to main base. This started the exodus of personnel and facilities off The Hill.

In September 1982, the Air Force announced plans to bring Air Force aircraft back to this strategically located base and deployed two squadrons of F-16s to Misawa for a short TDY.

I arrived back in Misawa in September of 1982.

In 1983 Col Smith accepted the coveted Travis Trophy for the 6920th ESG.

On 1 September 1983 a Russian fighter aircraft shot down Korean Air Lines Flight 007 north of Hokkaido. 269 lives were lost. The Air Force moved F15 fighters from Kadena Air Base, Okinawa to Misawa until tensions died down. Hill personnel were deployed to sites on Hokkaido to help in recovery efforts.

In November, JASDF activated its Interim Early Warning Air Group, the 601st Squadron.

The winter of 1983/84 set a record for snowfall. Misawa experienced 239.4 inches of snow.

In July 1984 the 432nd TFW assumed command of the base from the 6112th ABG.

The 1984 base Snow Festival was the last one that I can't find any mention of in the Northern Light so I assume it was the last one held.

PCF
Bldg. 1522

Aerial Photo of Security Hill circa 1985

The small, circular, white structures in the lower portion of the photo are the radomes that housed the satellite antennas.

Notice the Ladylove Permanent Collection Facility, bldg. 1522, which was completed in 1984. Ladylove operations had been ongoing for a few years in the Interim Collection Facility which was a small area on the south side of Building 1500 adjacent to the Navy operations area. However the move to the PCF provided a long-awaited, state of the art collection and processing center.

Ladylove Patch

On 1 January 1985, the 432nd TFW assumed control of the base flight line. The Naval Air Facility, Misawa was responsible for airfield operations since the 347th TFW departed in 1971.

5 April 1985 saw the first of the newly activated 13th TFS's F-16 arrive at Misawa. The rest of the squadron arrived incrementally over the next few months. The activation of this unit was said to level the playing field in numbers of fighter aircraft in the north Pacific area compared to potential enemies in the region. In April of 1985, the dollar value was down 152 yen.

The 1985 Spouse Open House included a first-ever tour of a sanitized portion of the HF Ops Floor.

In September of 1985, the Far East Network at Misawa moved their signal from Channel 73 to Channel 66. Federal Communications Commission rules changed and the frequency capability of newly produced American televisions would only go as high as 66 in the UHF spectrum.

The 1 April 1986 issue of the Northern Light bemoaned a further drop in the value of the dollar as the yen was down to 140 to the dollar.

In early 1986, the unit decided to dedicate its buildings to the memory of USAFSS personnel who were killed in action. A request to ESC Headquarters in San Antonio resulted in the names of five Security Service airmen who died during the same Airborne Radio Direction Finding mission when their EC47 aircraft was shot down during the Vietnam conflict. It should be noted that none of these airmen had ever been stationed in Misawa but qualified because they were Security Service members.

After many months of preparation and practice, on 11 November 1987, the unit held a Memorialization Ceremony. The building dedication list is below:

Building 1500 to TSgt. Louis Cleaver, Airborne Morse Systems Operator;

Building 1522 to SSgt. James Dorsey; Airborne Morse Systems Operator;

Building 1523 to TSgt. Rodney Gott, Airborne Morse Systems Operator;

Building 1574 to SSgt. Michael Conner, Airborne Morse Systems Operator;

Building 1523 Conference Room to Sgt. Clarence McNeill Airborne Voice Systems Operator.

Family members of TSgt Cleaver accepted the invitation to attend the ceremony which included a reading of the memorialization orders at each facility, Pass in Review by the 6 elements of the unit (four flights, daze and LG), a dedication speech by CMSgt Ron Schofield and a Missing Man Fly-by of F16s from the base's 432nd TFW. The five plaques that were affixed to the respective buildings are below. I apologize for the different sizes. This is not intended to try and show that any one is more significant than the others. It is simply that these are the best photos I could find for each airman.

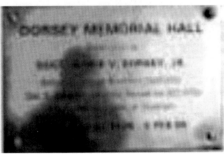

Operation Eyesight continued its special mission and in 1988 made their largest donation so far when they presented the Hachinohe School for the Blind and Deaf a check for 1.5 million yen ($12,500). A large part of this amount was gleaned from the first (and only) celebrity auction. Unit members contact numerous sports and motion picture/TV organizations, asking for donations of memorabilia and included information about Eyesight. The response was quite gratifying and the auction earned over $5,000. Thanks to the plunging yen exchange rate, this was not the most yen donated but was the highest dollar amount ever. There had once been a 2 million yen donation but the yen exchange rate was considerably more favorable at that time.

In January of 1989, Japanese Emperor Hirohito died after 62 years of rule. He was the longest reigning monarch in recorded history. He was succeeded by Crown Prince Akihito who, as of this writing, is in the 28th year of his reign.

1989 also saw the introduction of the Battle Dress Uniform (BDU, jungle camouflage pattern) which replaced the standard fatigues. In March of 1987 the long-awaited new BX, food court and concession mall opened. Shopping capacity more than tripled overnight. This year, Edgren High School graduated 47 seniors. As the year ended, you get 136 yen to the dollar.

Finally in 1989, the Enlisted Performance Report replaced the Airman Performance Report.

The population of Misawa City in 1990 was 42,303. The 3d Space Surveillance Squadron was assigned to Misawa in April. In May, the U.S. Navy returned control of Ripsaw bombing range to the Air Force. In December, the Yen rate was 136 to the dollar.

In 1990 Operation Eyesight donated ¥2,000,000 ($16,000) to the Hachinohe School for the Blind and Deaf. This allowed the school to buy two braille computers.

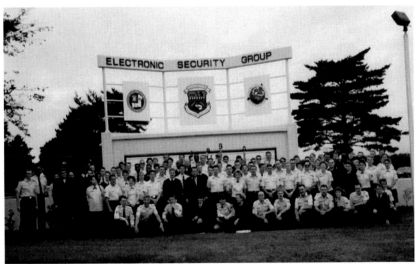

Security Hill Welcome Marquee – 1990

On 19 May 1991 E-4 Senior Airmen-NCOs will no longer be designated an E-4 NCO after one year time-in-grade. The Air Force determined that E-4 would have NCO status removed and the rank became Senior Airman for the duration of the member's time as an E-4.

Seems the only sure thing in the Air Force is that nothing is for sure. I often wondered how the service would build significant traditions if the rules keep changing.

In mid-June 1991 Mount Pinatubo, an active volcano, near Clark AB, Republic of the Philippines suffered a major eruption. Misawa, like other bases donated a significant amount of money and material to the victims of the eruption. The ash and debris fallout from this eruption was so great that the U.S. ended it presence at Clark Air Base later in 1991. Some of the personnel from the 6922nd ESG at Clark were reassigned to The Hill, increasing the population slightly.

On 3 October 1991 Electronic Security Command was replaced by the Air Force Intelligence Command. This change combined Electronic Security Command with the Air Force Special Activities Center and the Foreign Technology Division, both of which were sections of the Air Force Intelligence Agency. However, at least for the time being, the AF unit on The Hill remained 6920th ESG. Here is the command's patch.

AFIC Shield

Also in October, Typhoon Marielle snuck up the east coast of Japan and dealt Misawa a serious blow. Wind speeds reached over 90 miles per hour and damage included uprooted trees, lost roofing shingles and downed power lines. This is the strongest storm to reach Misawa in my 30-plus years here.

In June of 1992 the Army Field Station, Misawa drastically reduced its manning going from about 130 assigned to only 35.

Also in June of 92, the Yen hit a new high and was trading at 124 to the dollar.

I retired from the Air Force in July of 92 after 24 years of service.

In October 1992 operations on The Hill became "joint" with the Air Force, Navy and what was left of the Army and Marine presence working much more closely together. This began a new era of cooperation and sharing. This was the first joint operation in the world's cryptologic community. The operation became known as the Misawa Cryptologic Operations Center (MCOC). The Air Force maintained host responsibilities with the commander of the Air Force contingent as the director of the MCOC.

Hill Welcome Marquee – 1992

In January of 1993 another earthquake rocked Northern Japan. The quake was centered off the south-east coast of Hokkaido and registered 7.5.

53

Misawa City reported about $500,000.00 worth of damage in the form of broken pipes, damaged stores and broken windows. The base did not suffer any serious damage.

By June of 1993 the Yen had nosed-dived to 110 to the dollar. The Cost Of Living Allowance (COLA) covered most of the loss for Active Duty and DoD Civilians. We retirees who, of course, don't receive a COLA were forced to tighten our belts considerably.

In August of 1993, the Air Force once again revamped the Air Force Specialty Codes. The 207, 202, 203 intelligence career fields now use the 1N series. For example a 203X1 became a 1N3X1 a 207X1 became 1N2X1 and a 202X0 became a 1N4X1 (I think).

On 1 October 1993 the short-lived Air Force Intelligence Command became the Air Intelligence Agency (AIA). The 6920th ESG was inactivated and the operational unit on The Hill became the 301st Intelligence Squadron (IS). This activity occurred throughout the command. This marked the end of the 69XX unit designations that were used exclusively by USAFSS and ESC units. Note the Guidon Bearer in the Change of Command ceremony photo below is A1C William Couret.

Air Intelligence Agency

301st IS

The MCOC earned the Travis Trophy in 1993 as a joint operation. Another trophy was earned when Mrs. Joan Lindsey, wife of Hill Air Force MSgt Walter Lindsey won the Joan Orr Air Force Wife of the Year award for 1993.

By March of 94, the value of the Yen had climbed to only 98 to the dollar.

In October 1994 the 432nd Fighter Wing on main base was deactivated and the 35th Fighter Wing assumed control of the base. The new unit still operated F-16s. Also this month the new base hospital opened with many more specialists permanently assigned. This was a long-awaited and welcomed event.

On 4 October 1994 a major earthquake struck off the coast of Hokkaido but damage in the Misawa area was minimal.

The Entry Control Point in 1994

1994 also brought the Air Force contingent on The Hill another Travis Trophy. (The U.S. Naval Security Detachment, Misawa earned the award in 1974, 79 and 87. The U.S. Army Field Station, Misawa was presented the trophy in 1980.)

In March 1995 the Air Force took over all maintenance of the "Golf Ball" antennas from the contractor that maintained them up to this point.

In June of 1996, the 35th FW's F-16s were designated as the Air Force's only Wild Weasel squadron. They wear the WW on the vertical stabilizer and go in first to neutralize enemy anti-aircraft radars.

In September the new Club Tohoku opened to replace the Enlisted Club that was originally the Rocker Club as the base's enlisted open mess.

On 30 May, 1997 the 301st IS paid tribute to Sgt. Joseph Matejov who is the only USAFSS member who served on The Hill that was killed in action in Vietnam. The original Operations Building, bldg. 1555, was renamed Matejov Community Center. I had the privilege to attend the memorialization ceremony.

301st IS pays tribute to fallen comrades

by 1st Lt. Jason Lamont
301st IS
Misawa Air Base, Japan

The 301st Intelligence Squadron at Misawa Air Base, Japan, paid tribute to two fellow comrades who were killed in action during the Vietnam War by dedicating two buildings to their memory May 30.

The community center was renamed Matejov Community Center in honor of Sgt. Joseph Matejov, an airborne morse systems operator, who died when his EC-47 was shot down Feb. 5, 1973.

The 301st IS dormitory was renamed Ryon Hall after Master Sgt. John W. Ryon, a radio communications analysis technician, who died when his EC-47 crashed Nov. 21, 1972.

Both servicemen were members of Detachment 3, 6994th Security Squadron, Nakhon Phanom Royal Thai Air Force Base, Thailand.

Making this Memorial Day ceremony an even more extraordinary event was the attendance of Matejov's mother and brother, Mary and Stephen. Mrs. Matejov flew to Misawa from Langley, Va., to attend the ceremony.

She spoke briefly about her son and unveiled the plaque that will adorn the entrance to the building.

Col. Tony Bair, 301st IS commander, read a letter sent to the 301st IS by one of Matejov's former squadron mates who served with him during the conflict. Tom Egan, who flew as an EC-47 navigator during Vietnam, also spoke at the memorialization was.

Following the dedication of the two buildings, the Misawa Air Base community gathered in a wing-wide retreat. The formation was addressed by Brig. Gen. Bruce Wright, Misawa Air Base commander, and concluded with an F-16 fly-by. ∎

Right, Col. Tony Bair, 301st IS commander, presents flag to Mary and Stephen Matejov.

Below is a photo of the dedication display in the lobby of building 1555. The display was moved to Heritage Hall when building 1555 was taken down.

The unit also dedicated their dormitory to MSgt John W. Ryan who was also killed in combat in Vietnam. The above article addresses this ceremony as well as Matejov's. I was unable to find any additional information about MSgt Ryan.

In 1997, former Misawa Installation Commander, General Michael Ryan became Air Force Chief of Staff. His father, General John Ryan, preceded him in the position by a generation.

Dec 28, 1998 a 7.4 earthquake struck with the epicenter at the same fault as the 1968 Great Shakes Day. The base residents suffered some minor damage to personal property but the area escaped any significant problems.

In the summer of 1999, JASDF's 3rd Air Wing began flying the Mitsubishi F-2.

On 1 January 2000 the Y2K bug scare passed with barely a whimper.

On 16 June 2000 U.S. Army Security Agency Detachment Misawa was renamed the 403^{rrd} Military Intelligence Detachment. Also, somewhere along this timeline, the Army Security Agency was renamed the U.S. Army Intelligence & Security Command (INSCOM).

On 16 September 2000 the 373rd Intelligence, Surveillance and Reconnaissance Group (373rd ISRG) was activated as host on The Hill. The 301st IS came under its control and the 373rd Spt. Sq. was also activated under the ISRG.

On 30 November 2000, the Marine Company E contingent ceased operations on The Hill and was deactivated.

During 2000 and early 2001, a group of active duty and retired individuals, led by CMSgt Jerry Gething put together Heritage Hall. This display of memorabilia had its Grand Opening in July of 2002 and resided inside building 1523, which was the "day shop" add-on to building 1500. It was a collection of ops equipment, photos, donated personal items and other links to The Hill's storied past. I never thought we would be the ones needing escorts.

Heritage Hall Main Aisle

MSgt (Ret) Don Ohman with his escort

Upon the later departure of the mission on The Hill, Heritage Hall memorabilia items were shipped to the unit's new home at Elmendorf AFB. Heritage Hall lives on at http://www.misawajapan.com/heritagehall/ .

On 1 July 2003 the Misawa Cryptologic Operations Center was renamed to the Misawa Security Operations Center (MSOC).

The MSOC earned another Travis Trophy in 2004, this time as a joint operation.

The base newspaper published its last issue at the end of December 2006 due to cost constraints. The base folks now get their news from http://misawa.af.mil. This web site is administered in the states so local Public Affairs folks were unable to provide archive versions for my research. This work from here on is compiled mostly from my memory with some help from my friends and The Hill's 60th Anniversary Committee.

In June 2007, Air Intelligence Agency became the Air Force Intelligence, Surveillance and Reconnaissance Agency however the 301st IS retained its designation as did the 373rd ISRG. This seems really confusing with the unit having a different designation from the parent agency but that's what my research showed. I truly hope I got it right.

On 11 March 2011 another huge earthquake with a magnitude of 9.3 rocked northeastern Japan. Fortunately for Misawa, the center was a couple of hundred miles south and offshore near the city of Fukushima in Miagi Prefecture. This quake generated a massive tsunami (tidal wave) that cost tens of thousands of lives and cost such a huge monetary figure that I won't attempt a guess. Fortunately, the giant wave lost most of its energy and only traveled about 30 yards from the normal shoreline at Misawa and caused very little damage. The base contributed thousands of man-hours to the rescue and recovery effort in and around Fukushima.

As for the Yen rate, there are no base papers so I can't give you an actual timeline but the Yen dropped as low as 73 to the dollar in the 2012/2013 timeframe. A national election in 2009 put a coalition of parties, led by the Democratic Party of Japan (DPJ), into power and the Liberal Democratic Party of Japan (LDP) lost control of the government for the first time since the end of World War II. Shortly after this election, the yen started to gain against the dollar and eventually the rate got to the mid-70s. It remained there for a few years. In 2012, another national election installed the Liberal Democratic Party back into power. Coincidently, soon after this election, the Yen began to steadily weaken. It is now January of 2016 and Yen rate is holding at about 115 to the dollar.

Aerial View of Security Hill in 2012

In the above photo, you can see that all of the old dorms are gone. Bldg. 1574, the command section building (the White House) is also gone. Bldg. 1555, Glenn Hall, the old Electron Theater (later known as the MEAR Team building) and some other old wooden buildings are all still there but won't be for long.

You can see that new modern buildings have been erected but they have nothing to do with the 301st IS except that some of them provide utilities to The Hill.

In January of 2013 the unit held a Security Hill 60th Anniversary Celebration. The theme was "Celebrating 60 Years of Vigilance". The affair was hosted by 373rd ISRG commander, Colonel Kimberly Joos. Dignitaries from the states, active duty and civilian personnel from Misawa and a number of us retirees attended.

64

In the photo above that's Joe Roginski standing at attention on the far right. Next to him is "Herman "T" Tinnerella and then the short guy is Toby Fanelli. That's me just behind Toby's right shoulder. Col Joos is front and center. Behind Col. Joos are Mr. Robin Blevins and Mr. Joel Austin. Other retirees in the photo are Cecil Hahn (just behind Col. Joos' right shoulder) and Don Oman half hidden in the rear. In the front row, to the left of Col. Joos, are Richard Masoner and Ronald Stark (U.S. Army). Barely visible behind Ron is Col. Paul Nelson, a former Security Hill Commander from 2007 to 2009. Our distinguished visitor is MGen Bob Otto in the mess dress on the far left. This bittersweet ceremony preceded the shutdown of ops by just a few months.

July 2013 marked the end of the collection and analysis on The Hill.

Hill Welcome Marquee, 2013

The 60 year period is commemorated with a simple monument that stands in the small field outside the compound's Entry Control Point, in the field where part of Bldg. 1555 once stood. Below is a photo of it.

While this marked the end of 60 years of operational mission, I chose to continue this narrative until the entire military presence on The Hill is terminated. This took place in July 2015.

The FLR-9 antenna was scheduled to be taken down in 2013 as there was no longer any need for its capabilities. However, due to limited funding, the demolition was delayed until December 2014.

While the actual mission moved in 2013, it wasn't until 30 June 2014, that the 301st IS Inactivation Ceremony was held at the Officers' Club. The unit moved to Joint Base Elmendorf/Richardson in Alaska and stood up at that location on 1 July 2014. Below are photos as the guidon is encased.

Please notice that the Guidon Bearer in these photos, CMSgt William Couret is the same person who held the guidon as an A1C in the 301st's 1991 activation ceremony pictured above.

301IS Inactivation Ceremony

This marked the end of USAF operational presence on Misawa's Security Hill as Lt Col Eric T. Monico surrendered the 301st IS guidon to 373rd ISRG commander, Col Joseph Winters. The 373rd ISRG and the 373rd Spt. Sq. remained active and were tasked with preparing the facilities and equipment for destruction or reutilization.

The U.S. Army Field Station, Misawa was deactivated in October of 2014 and the U.S. Navy Security Group Activity, Misawa stood down in November of 2014.

Also in October of 2014, Building 1555, the original operations building, later known as the Community Center, mail room, and Matejov Community Center was demolished.

Matejov Community Center (bldg. 1555) prior to its destruction
That's yours truly with the black jacket and Col. Kimberly Joos on the left who did so much to keep us old farts involved with happenings on The Hill. This photo is from 2013.

As things seriously wind down, Toby Fanelli and I decided we should probably get a photo with The Cage before it was gone forever. Here we are, below, at the last unit picnic in October 2014.

Demolition of the actual, above-ground, structure of the FLR-9 began in November of 2014 and was completed in May of 2015. Here are two photos taken on 4 December of 2014.

The above shot is from the softball field at the picnic area. As you can see, the entire A-B band reflecting screen is gone except for a few vertical support towers. This reflecting screen formed the outer structure that gave it the "elephant cage" look. All the shorter vertical B-band elements are down. The taller A-band elements and the C-band reflecting screen and elements are still standing but won't be for long.

The view from the top of the Ski Slope shows only a few of the elements left.

The photo below is a great shot by SFC Ronald Stark (Ret), U.S. Army Field Station, Misawa of the last antenna tower just before it was taken down. FYI, it's an A Band tower.

Last Warrior Standing

Finally, in May of 2015, the Cage was gone forever. As you can probably tell, the antenna was an iconic symbol to me and its passing merits special attention so please bear with me.

The empty space as seen from the common vantage point of the base ski slope

Another common view is from the base beach

In a ceremony on The Hill, outside the gig, the 373rd Spt. Gp. was deactivated on 2 June 2015 as Lt. Col. Jonathan M. Boling relinquished the unit's guidon to 373rd ISRG commander, Col Michael Winters. I was unable to get any photos of this ceremony.

On 12 June 2015, a Change of Responsibility ceremony was held as control of the MSOC transferred from military to civilian authorities.

The commander of the 373rd ISRG, Col Winters departed in July of 2014 marking the official end to the military presence on The Hill.

The population of Misawa's security hill now consisted of a small group of civilian caretakers/maintainers. Below is the latest aerial view of The Hill, taken in October of 2015. Note the area where the FLR-9 used to be looks a lot like the photo earlier in the book taken during the construction of the antenna.

This pictorial walk down memory lane has also come to an end. I sincerely hope you enjoyed this book as much as I enjoyed putting it together. I also hope that my amateurish writing efforts did not get in the way of your reading pleasure.

Loose Ends

There are a couple things that I was unable to find in my research that should have happened but eluded me. They are listed below.

I could not find any reference to the closing of The Hill mailroom and APO 96210. The service stopped prior to my second tour with began in 1982 and decades before they finally tore down its home, building 1555.

There were plenty of references to the AFN radio station being 1580 KHz but sometime in the 80s it moved to 1575 KHz where it remains today. I just can't tell you when.

Unit Awards

UNIT	AWARD	FROM	TO	DEVICES
1ST RSM	AFOUA	26 Nov 50	18 Jul 51	
6921SS	RVNGCWP	1 Apr 66	28 Jan 73	Palm
HQ 6921SW	AFOUA	1 Jul 67	30 Jun 68	
6921SS	AFOUA	1 Jan 68	31 Dec 69	Combat V
6921SW	AFOUA	1 Jan 68	31 Dec 69	
6921SS	AFOUA	1 Jan 70	31 Mar 71	Combat V
6921SS	AFOUA	1 Apr 71	31 Mar 72	Combat V
6921SW	AFOUA	j Jul 73	30 Jun 75	
6921SS	AFOUA	1 Jul 73	30 Jun 75	
6921SG	AFOUA	1 Jul 74	30 Jun 75	
6920SG	AFOUA	1 Jul 76	31 Dec 77	
6920SW	AFOUA	1 Jul 76	31 Dec 77	
HQ 6920SW	AFOUA	1 Jul 76	31 Dec 77	
6920ESG	AFOUA	1 Jul 82	30 Dec 84	
6920ESG	AFOUA	1 Jul 86	30 Jun 88	
6920ESG	AFOUA	1 Jul 91	30 Jun 93	
301IS	AFOUA	1 Oct 93	30 Sep 94	
301IS	AFOUA	1 Oct 94	30 Sep 95	
301IS	AFOUA	1 Oct 99	30 Sep 00	

UNIT	AWARD	FROM	TO	DEVICES
301IS	AFOUA	1 Jun 04	31 May 05	
301IS	AFOUA	6 Jun 08	31 May09	
301IS	AFOUA	1 Jan 10	31 Dec 10	
301IS	AFOUA	1 Jan 11	31 Dec 11	
301IS	AFOUA	31 Jan 12	31 Dec 12	

The 373 Support Group earned 4 AFOUAs, one with V Device

AFOUA

RVNCGWP

Legend:

AFOUA   Air Force Outstanding Unit Award

RVNCGWP   Republic of Vietnam Cross of Gallantry with Palm device

RSM   Radio Squadron (Mobile)

SS   Security Squadron

HQ   Head Quarters

SW   Security Wing

SG   Security Group

ESG   Electronic Security Group

IS   Intelligence Squadron

Data courtesy of the Air Force Personnel Center's Awards DMZ web site and www.homeofheros.com

Unit Commanders

The commanders on The Hill listed below are the men and women who commanded the Security Hill host unit. In some cases they were the commander of a squadron and at other times they commanded a group or wing that consisted of squadrons which actually did the collection, analysis and maintenance mission.

Commander's Name	Inclusive Dates	Unit
Lt Col Charles W. Shepard	Jul 51 - Nov 53	1st RSM
Lt Col J. W. Brady	Nov 53 – Feb 55	1st RSM
Maj William H. Madole	Feb 55 – Apr 55	6921RSM
Lt Col Charles D. Pryor	Apr 55 – May 55	6921RSM
Maj William H. Madole	May 55 – Sep 56	6921RSM/RGM
Lt. Col James S. Novy	Sep 56 – Dec 57	6921RGM
Col Gerald E. Branch	Dec 57 – Sep 59	6921RGM
Col Dale S. Seeds	Sep 59 – Sep 60	6921RGM
Col James F. Berry	Sep 60 – Aug 62	6921RGM
Col Adolph M. Wright	Aug 62 – Jul 63	6921SW
Col Kenneth W. Davey *	Jul 63 – Aug 63	6921SW
Col Gordon W. Wildes	Aug 63 – Jul 64	6921SW
Col Kenneth W. Davey	Jul 64 – Jun 66	6921SW
Col Thomas J. Hanley III	Jun 66 – Mar 68	6921SW
Col Harry A. Wilson	Mar 68 – Jun 69	6921SW
Col Leonard M Legge **	Jun 69 – Jan 70	6921SW

Commander's Name	Inclusive Dates	Unit
Col Cary A. Thompson	Jan 70 – May 70	6921SG
Lt Col Robert W. Shively	May 70 – Jun 70	6921SG
Col Charles F. Beatie, Jr.	Jun 70 – Nov 72	6921SG
Col Robert H. Touby	Dec 72 – Apr 74	6921SW
Col Charles J. Luther	Apr 74 – Jun 74	6920SG
Col John F. Grant	Jun 75 – Jul 75	6920SG
Lt Col John G. Hennessey	Aug 75 – May 78	6920SG
Lt. Col Juan F. Lopez	May 78 – Jun 80	6920SS/6920ESG
Col Terry E. Heath	Jul 80 – Jun 82	6920ESG
Col Allan T. Smith	Jun 82 – Jun 84	6920ESG
Col Joseph P. Burchfield	Jul 84 – Jun 86	6920ESG
Col Calvin Murphy	Jul 86 – Jun 88	6920ESG
Col Douglas Williams	Jul 88 – Jun 91	6920ESG
Col Michael McFarland	Jul 91 – Jul 93	6920ESG
Col Arthur J. Saitta	Jul 93 – Jul 95	6920ESG/301IS
Col Joseph Hurst	Jul 95 – Jun 96	301IS/MCOC
Col Warren Miller ***	Jul 96 – Dec 97	301IS/MCOC
Col Wyatt C Cook	Jan 98 – Jun 99	301IS/MCOC
Col Dennis Mitzel	Aug 99 – Jun 02	373ISRG/MCOC
Col Fred W. Gortler	Jun 02 – Jan 04	373ISRG/MSOC
Col Gary Bender	Jan 04 – Aug 05	373ISRG/MSOC

Commander's Name	Inclusive Dates	Unit
Col Joseph L. Hollett	Aug 05 – Oct 05	373ISRG/MSOC
Lt Col Cheryl A. Kearney	Oct 05 – Jan 06	373ISRG/MSOC
Col Elise M. Vandervennet	Jan 06 – Aug 07	373ISRG/MSOC
Col Paul D. Nelson	Aug 07 – Jul 09	373ISRG/MSOC
Col Barry Leister	Jul 09 – Jul 11	373ISRG/MSOC
Col Kimberlee P. Joos	Jul 11- Jun 13	373ISRG/MSOC
Col Michael J. Winters	Jun 13 – Jul 15	373ISRG/MSOC

* In Aug of 1962, Colonel Davy temporarily assumed command while awaiting the arrival of Colonel Wildes

** Colonel Legge died suddenly of a heart attack on 20 Jan 1970.

*** The exact months of command for from 1997 through 2005 (with the exception of Col. Cook's tenure) are possibly off slightly. The information I gathered for this period was confusing. No single document covered this timeframe completely. I have tried to 202 it (analyze) but I have not found definitive proof that the months are accurate.

Note: Information in this section was provided by a document originally compiled by HQ/ESC in Dec 1984; Mr. Andrew W. Anthony, the 70 ISRW historian; and a thorough perusal of archive copies of the Northern Light and the Wingspread base newspapers, courtesy of the 35FW Historian, Dr. Dennis H. Clark. Capt. Reyne Hochstein and SSgt Joshua Eggum of the 301st IS were extremely helpful in tracking down this information.

Commanders above reflect those who commanded the host unit.

Do You Remember?

Below is a list of all the things I can remember that bring back memories. They are listed in no particular order. Most of them have been cancelled, closed, discontinued or went away by attrition. If you remember something you see here, I hope it brings a smile to your lips. Some of these things were exclusive to Misawa and others were widely used. Enjoy.

360 Yen to the Dollar

AFRTS – FEN (currently AFN - Armed Forces Network – still active.)

After last mid Roll Calls

After-swing Bowling

AP Alley, (Toy's, The Trick, New Tokyo, The Metro, Companions, The Bacchus (ju yen blackjack), The Deuce, The Neutral, Top Hat) Saki Alley, Critter Alley, Chisai Alley, Covered Alley

Base Level Sports (Permissive TDY to play ball and represent Misawa against the likes of Johnson AB, Chitose AB, Tachikawa AB, Yokota AB, Brady AS, Fuchu AB, Naha AB, Shiroi AB and others. This went away in the early 70s)

Base Snow Festival

Beggar Bennies

Changee Cheets (Linen exchange)

China Pete's and Pony's

Comfy Olympics (still active elsewhere?)

Ebina Electric Shop

Golden Flow

Jeep Jokes (Sweeping Snow from the FLR-9 elements, counting chad, dodging radio waves, etc)

Komaki's Kappa Festival (This went away in the 90s as Komaki Onsen came under new management.)

MARS (Military Affiliate Radio Station)

No boots on the Ops Floor. Sneakers only.

Omisawa and Furamaki. (The part of town outside the main gate was called Omisawa and the area around the train station was called Furimaki. It was like the two areas were separate communities and not all part of Misawa as we've known it since at least the late 60s.)

Operation Eyesight food booth

Over-30 Intramural Sports

Pin-Up Girls in the Wingspread (Marilyn Monroe, Jayne Mansfield, Bridget Bardot and many, many more. Had 'em til the early 70s)

Pokes!

Red Feather (till active)

Roll Calls (in the alley)

"Second Show" (2 Chuo) and Yurakuza Theaters. Gone in the late 70s.

Static Club, Circuit Breaker, Electron Theater (all gone years ago)

Studded snow tires. Man, did they tear up the road. They were outlawed in Japan in 1991. Now the Japanese call snow tires "studless".

Sweeping Snow from the FLR-9 elements, counting chad, dodging radio waves

The Far East Network's 72-hour Youth Disc-athon. A fund raising event where challenges are made over the air and could be performed or paid off by exceeding the challenge amount. I remember challenging The Hill commander to allow us to wear civvies on a set of mids for a donation. Later on, done for Red Feather also.

TOPS (Take Off Pounds Sensibly)

Z.I. (Zone of the Interior. More recently called CONUS or Continental U.S.)

Bonus

Here is a link to my website that displays photos that just would not fit into this book. Some are of The Hill and others are of main base and downtown that I thought would spark some memories.   I will try to add to these photos as I get new ones so check the page from time to time. Hope you get a little nostalgic. Enjoy!

http://www.misawajapan.com/book_bonus/book_bonus.asp

About the Author (in Misawa)

The closing of The Hill was a shock to me. I spent 13 years working in building 1500. I was here from September of 1970 until September 1973 as a 292X1/207X1 working in Block 1 and then in DF (great job) on Trick 4.

I returned in 1982 and my first position was SMSS of Baker Flight. (Why did they get rid of the Trick 1 through 4 names?) I kind of liked them and felt it made Misawa unique for an Air Force unit.)

I spent the final ten years of my Air Force career here on The Hill in a variety of positions. Upon retirement, I was Superintendent of Mission Management (DOM) and the Far East HFDF Network. I retired from the Air Force here at Misawa in July 1992 and really retired in October of 2013. I still live here in Oirase Chou which neighbors Misawa to the south. It used to be called Shimoda.

If you know what an SMSS and HFDF are then you were here a while ago. SMSS is Senior Morse Systems Supervisor and HFDF is High Frequency Direction Finding. There used to be a Senior Printer Systems Supervisor (SPSS), Mission Supervisor and Surveillance &Warning Supervisor (S&W) as well.

If you ever get back to Misawa, look me up. I'll be volunteering at the Retiree Activities Office here on the base.

Made in the USA
Middletown, DE
10 February 2017